Straight Pipes

Devotions for BIKERS

ISBN: 1-59872-740-0

Promises for Bikers

The Message

Psalm 46:10 - *Step out of the traffic! Take a long loving look at Me, Your High God above politics, above everything.* No matter how busy we are, how many rallies we go to, or how many people we minister to, God wants us to stop what we are doing to meet with Him. He promises to be there.

Jeremiah 29:11 - *I know what I'm doing. I have it all planned out–plans to take care of you, not abandon you, plans to give you the future you hope for.* God has a purpose for your life—a good purpose. Rest in His plans.

Joshua 1:9 – *Haven't I commanded you? Strength! Courage! Don't be timid; don't get discouraged. God, your God, is with you every step you take.* In every step we take God is ready to walk beside us, even carry us when we are too weak to walk alone.

Romans 8:1 – *Those who enter into Christ's being-here-for-us no longer have to live under a continuous, low-lying black cloud. A new power is in operation.* Sin and death no longer have a hold on the person who's relinquished his life to Christ's control.

Psalm 119: 105 – *By Your Words I can see where I'm going; they throw a beam of light on my dark path.* God's Word illuminates the dark corners of our lives, and He, living in us, shines brightly into crowds of people who think we are everywhere, even when our numbers are few.

2 Chronicles 16:9 – *God is always on the alert, constantly on the lookout for people who are totally committed to Him. You are foolish to go for human help when you could have had God's help.* God knows when your heart is committed to doing things His way, and He commits to you in return, to provide the help you need when you are in a troubling situation.

James 1:5 – *If you don't know what you're doing, pray to the Father. He loves to help. You'll get His help, and won't be condescended to when you ask for it.* God will give you the wisdom you need the moment you need it, willingly, not making you feel less of a person for asking.

Proverbs 3: 5-6 – *Trust God from the bottom of your heart; don't try to figure out everything on your own. Listen for God's voice in everything you do, everywhere you go; He's the one who will keep you on track.* To trust "from the bottom of your heart" means to put the weight of whatever you're doing on His shoulders. Let Him guide and direct, for He wants only the best for you.

Romans 15:4 – *God wants the combination of His steady, constant calling and warm, personal counsel in Scripture to come to characterize us, keeping us alert for whatever He will do next.* God wants you to gain confidence by reading His Word, learning how He has been faithful in the past so that you will know He has promised to be faithful in the days ahead.

Matthew 7:11 – *As bad as you are....you're at least decent to your own children. So don't you think the God who conceived you in love will be even better?* If humans can be kind, imagine how kind God, the Creator of kindness, can be. God understands, cares, and comforts us individually because He knows us as individuals.

Christianity is a heart issue, not a tradition, a means of keeping the Law of Moses, or an opportunity to work our way into heaven. God deals directly with our Christian belief, but in order for Him to work in our lives, we need to be spending time with Him on a regular basis.

This devotional is designed to encourage bikers in their Christian walk and, at the same time, provide them with a tool to disciple others. All verses are taken from the New International Version of the Bible (NIV).

Prayer: What is it, and what does the Bible have to say about our prayer life?

The next few pages will help you discover exactly what God calls prayer, how we can adopt a regular prayer life, and why we should.

NOTES

Rally Near Him

What other nation is so great as to have their gods near them the way the Lord our God is near us whenever we pray to him (Deut. 4:7).

Christians have an awesome privilege. God is listening. Jesus is intervening… when we pray, seeking His answers for life situations. Each morning, before the hustle and bustle of daily life gets in the way, we have the opportunity to sit down with the God of the Universe, our Creator, and visit about the situations, pressures, trials, and burdens we face.

An easy formula to follow is the word **ACTS (Adore, Confession, Thanksgiving, and Supplication)**. Before we rev up the motorcycle, we can worship Him (**A**dore) from the sanctity of our home, renewing our relationship with His Holy Spirit for the day ahead. We can **C**onfess the mistakes we've made and take care of anything that might stand in the way of God hearing our pleas. We can seek His forgiveness. We can **T**hank Him personally, for everything about our life is pure pleasure, balm for a believing heart. Then we seek His answers for ourselves and others (**S**upplication), leaving burdensome worries at His feet. That takes the pressure off, as long as we're truly willing to accept His solutions.

Motorcycle riders have no idea where God will use their bikes to open doors of ministry. We enjoy the freedom of the wind touching our bodies, the freedom from the four-wheel cage. But, as Christians, we know that Jesus commanded us to "Go out into all the world. ..." The first step is to listen for God's plan. Listen to see where He wants us, and where He is already working. We aren't in a position to listen if we're not allowing His Holy Spirit to work in our heart through daily prayer and Bible study. Begin this morning. Set aside a short time, in a quiet place, to seek God's face. Then listen and ride.

NOTES

NOTES

God Connections

As for me, far be it from me that I should sin against the Lord by failing to pray for you (1 Sam. 12:23a).

The people asked Samuel to pray for them. Have you ever stopped to gas up the bike and had the opportunity to pray for someone but didn't do it right then? Oh, you said, "I'll pray for you." However, as soon as something else down the road caught your attention, you forgot all about that hurting soul. The people in Samuel's day had sinned. They wanted Samuel to intervene on their behalf, to pray for them. Samuel agreed and did so, on the spot, an example we all should follow.

It is amazing how many non-Christian bikers will allow us to pray for them. When we visit with a biker at a rest stop along the highway, in front of the gas pumps, or at a rally, we can pray right there for their hurts and needs. That's a "God Appointment." When we ask them if we can pray for them, as Samuel points out, to just walk away and forget them is sin in God's eyes. WOW!

Add them to your prayer list as well, so when you meet with God each morning, you can continue to lift them up before the throne. Keep track of the people God places in your path and pray for them daily. You don't even have to know all the details of their lives to effectively pray and ask God to intervene, to open their hearts. While it is immensely important that we pray with them as soon as they agree to it, it is also important that we continue to place them before the altar of God.

Begin keeping track of the people God brings into your sphere of influence. You may never run into them again, but for as long as they is on your heart, pray diligently and fervently. God will let you know when to stop.

NOTES

NOTES

Holy Spirit Courage

Pray in the Spirit on all occasions with all kinds of prayers and requests. With this in mind, be alert and always keep on praying for all the saints (Eph. 6:18).

John was tenacious. He loved the Lord with a powerful resolve to share his faith with everyone he met. John came out of the outlaw culture because someone cared enough to pray for him, to share the faith with him, and he allowed the Holy Spirit to change his life.

The Holy Spirit is a gift to us from Jesus Christ, presented first for the disciples when He ascended into heaven and then again when the early Church was adding to its numbers, as seen in Acts. The Holy Spirit is God, the third Person of the Trinity, and yet we often completely ignore His work in our lives.

One of His tasks is to help us pray for people. He knows better that any of us what a particular person needs in his or her life. He knows what it will take to bring that person relief or into a closer personal relationship with God the Father. Relying on the Spirit or praying in the Spirit makes perfect sense.

Bikers often have short conversations with other motorcycle enthusiasts. We may never meet them again, but for that short time God has placed us in a position to minister to them. Paul tells us in the book of Romans that everyone sins and needs God's intervention and forgiveness, not just the long-haired, tattooed biker who happens to pull up to the other side of the gas pump.

Very few people will refuse prayer on their behalf. Quietly, within the confines of your heart, ask the Holy Spirit to give you the words, and then watch what happens. Gaze at a hardened face turned soft when God ministers to a heart through the prayer of an obedient servant.

NOTES

NOTES

Club Dues

Hear the supplication of your servant and of your people Israel when they pray toward this place. Hear from heaven, your dwelling place, and when you hear, forgive
(1 Kings 8:30).

Solomon stood before the altar of God, raised his hands toward heaven in front of the people of Israel, and spoke these words in a long prayer of dedication for the temple he had just built. He acknowledged that God could not be contained, even in the highest heaven or in that temple. This verse reveals Solomon's recognition of the importance of prayer. He understood how significant it was for God to forgive His people, because His people were far from perfect.

Derek was amazed. His life had been interspersed with booze, women, and drugs. He'd committed many punishable offenses and had even served a short term in prison. Yet God forgave him, and the Holy Spirit indwelled him. For the first time in his life, Derek felt he was worth something. Derek discovered God's redeeming love because another motorcycle rider dared to pray for him. Derek joined God's club.

While God can't be enclosed, it is amazing that He is willing to live in the hearts

NOTES

of His people. He forgives eagerly, and His Spirit indwells us because He loves us. He covers us with His grace, making it possible for us to have a personal relationship with Him, and it's important that we take care of that relationship on a daily basis.

How do you maintain a close friendship with people? Do you ignore them? Do you spend as little time as possible with them? Hardly. You look forward to sitting under a large oak tree with them to swap stories, or gathering together at a member's house. You all wear the same identifying marks, whether back patches or tattoos. You're a family.

Derek became part of God's family. He hungered for that time each morning when he could sit in God's presence before jumping on his bike and going to work. Why not spend time regularly with the One who loves you far more than anyone ever could, who longs for your attention, who finds joy in forgiving your repentant heart?

NOTES

Clean House

If my people, who are called by my name, will humble themselves and pray and seek my face and turn from their wicked ways, then will I hear from heaven and will forgive their sin and will heal their land (2 Chron. 7:14).

Solomon, in this chapter of the Bible, is once again asking God to forgive the wickedness of His people. He pleads their case just as a lawyer defends his client. God lays down conditions for His forgiveness. He wants His people to humble themselves. He asks us to admit our sins, to pray and ask for forgiveness, to seek Him continually, and to turn from our sinful behavior. He wants us to show true repentance by our changed behavior.

God has not changed His mind, ever. He is a sovereign God, just and holy. Sin separates us from Him. He requires true repentance, a changed heart, and changed attitudes. What happens when we let small repairs on a motorcycle go? They turn into big, expensive repairs. The same happens with sin. If we don't take care of the smallest sin, it grows into something that takes a long time to change.

Debra took care of the sin in her life on a daily basis. She was able to focus on yesterday's sin more easily than she could remember the things she'd neglected all month. If not dealt with on a regular basis, sins pile up—like that delinquent gas bill from too many road trips. Debra understood that. Her faith-walk led her away from the outlaws she'd been hanging with and closer to other Christians who became her new role models. They taught her to keep a clean house, and to take care of business quickly and on a daily basis.

If this aspect of the Christian life were not important, God would not spend so much time in the Bible telling us to repent and sin no more. Allow the Holy Spirit to convict you of a wrongdoing as soon as you've done it. Then confess it, seek forgiveness, and turn from that behavior.

NOTES

NOTES

First Things First

After He had dismissed them, He went up on a mountainside by Himself to pray. When evening came, He was there alone (Matt. 14:23).

Jesus had just ministered to a multitude of people. They hung on His every word, an exhausting responsibility for the Lord. How did He choose to refurbish His stamina, His strength? Not by getting a good night's sleep, but by praying. In fact, He spent a long time in prayer. He was still on His knees into the night.

How can we expect to minister to God's people anywhere we meet them and yet neglect our prayer life? How can we expect to have the strength to listen to lost souls, pray for them, and then love them unconditionally if we don't bask in the light of God's love at least once a day?

Many times we return from some motorcycle event exhausted from physical labor, spiritual warfare, and lack of sleep. It is important to have people at home praying for us through those events, but it is also important that we seek the Lord before, during, and after.

You may think you are not confronting the enemy when you ride your motorcycle, but if you are looking for God's appointments on the highways and byways, you can count on the enemy draining you spiritually. Spend time with God every day. Ask Him to show you where He wants you to go. Allow the Holy Spirit to flow over you. He energizes, strengthens, and renews your spirit for the day ahead.

.

NOTES

NOTES

Biker Blessing

Then little children were brought to Jesus for him to place his hands on them and pray for them (Matt. 19:13a).

Jesus prayed for others, even the least significant among His followers. He rebuked His disciples for trying to send the children away because He knew those little ones needed His prayers. Jesus is our example. He prayed for people everywhere, anytime, and under all circumstances. He was not too important to spend time with children, men, or women. The hurting, as well as the deformed and disease-ridden, came to Him.

People cross our path every time we ride a motorcycle. Some are crude and rude, but all need to know that Jesus loves them. Some are bikers, but many are just inquisitive about motorcycles, the tool God uses to catch their attention. We meet them at a convenience store, at gas stations, or in parking lots. Their curiosity about riding overrules their timidity as they approach us to ask how the ride is going, where we've been, and where we're going.

A door has opened. We listen as they tell us a little about themselves, but then we ask, "Can I pray for you?" This biker blessing comes from God as He puts words in our mouth. He places His hand on the head of those we pray for, and His love flows through us to touch the heart of a lost soul.

This God appointment will bypass you if you have not taken the time to sit at His feet before you leave for the ride. Seek His face. Ask for forgiveness for your independence from Him. With boldness, He will give you the courage to share His gospel, His Bible, or His tracts—tools you carry for just that purpose. Walking in the Holy Spirit helps you focus on others when you stop for a cold drink of water on a blazing-hot day, or to stretch sore muscles. Gain strength today from a daily appointment with God, and then walk in His Spirit to see where He's already working.

NOTES

NOTES

Turning Ourselves In

Therefore let everyone who is godly pray to you...(Ps. 32:6a).

David, in this Psalm, describes a time when he was silent before the Lord. During his silence, his bones wasted away, but when he admitted or acknowledged his sins to God, God forgave his disobedience. His sense of peace was restored.

Ben robbed a convenience store last night. Wendy stole some money from her mother's purse. Vicki lied to her husband about where the money from their bank account had gone. Tom gazed upon his young neighbor with longing in his eyes while his wife made dinner inside their home. Their conscience bothered them. It niggled at them for days, like a bad taste coats the inside of your mouth, until each one finally fell on their knees before God. It doesn't matter what the sin is; you won't feel restored until you've repented before God. He even gives you the courage to go to the authorities if necessary.

By praying to God and confessing our sins, we recognize that He has the right to pronounce our actions corrupt, evil, and wicked. He's the judge. We realize that what we have done, even the desire to do it, is wrong. We announce our intention to abandon that particular transgression in order to follow Him more closely.

The desire of every Christian's heart should be to walk closely in the footsteps of our Savior, to follow His example. Along the way, however, the path becomes rocky and we sometimes slip off. Trying to hide our mistakes, as Adam and Eve did in the garden, is like a fish in a fish bowl trying to hide from prying eyes.

Not just once a week on Sunday, but every day, seek Him in the morning, as you walk through your day, and before you go to bed at night. Restore that most important of all relationships by confessing and receiving forgiveness.

NOTES

NOTES

Biker Law

Now when Daniel learned that the decree had been published, he went home to his upstairs room where the windows opened toward Jerusalem. Three times a day he got down on his knees and prayed, giving thanks to his God, just as he had done before (Dan. 6:10).

In this country we have a hard time thinking of a place where we can't pray or believe in God and worship Him. In Daniel's day a decree was issued that anyone who prayed to any god except the king would be thrown into the lion's den—a death sentence. When we go to a rally, there are rules. Some rules are good, for our own protection, while others ask us to compromise our faith. In this passage Daniel remained loyal to God, and God protected him.

Daniel prayed before an open window. He faced the death penalty and yet had the courage to do what he knew God wanted. When standing in a parking lot, do you fear that someone may see you praying for the smelly, homeless person? What about the biker couple who just pulled up on a Gold Wing? Are you afraid people will think you're not cool if you strike up a conversation with them?

Fear can paralyze. It can make us ineffective just when God has opened a door or brought someone by who especially needs Him at that moment. Satan is the author of fear. Reject him, and then draw on God's courage to build a relationship, no matter how fleeting. Be sensitive to those people God places in your path. Follow His Spirit's leading, and then go do the right thing

NOTES

NOTES

Biker Culture

But I tell you: Love your enemies and pray for those who persecute you (Matt. 5:44).

Barbara did not love bikers. In fact, she was flabbergasted that any Christian would go into that culture to eat with them, laugh with them, and love them. God had other plans. Standing on a rock-strewn mountainside, with the sun's rays beating down on Him, Jesus taught thousands of people, including His disciples, to love their enemies and to pray for those who persecuted them. Bikers weren't persecuting her, but God changed Barbara's heart. She began to see them through God's eyes. He loved them, created them, and died for them, just as He had for her.

God asks us to love our enemies, to pray for them, and to forgive them. Someone in a car or a van doesn't look where he is driving; he pulls out in front of a biker on the highway, sending him and his cycle screeching down the pavement. The biker winds up in the ditch with a multitude of scrapes and bruises, broken bones, and lacerations. His motorcycle is totaled, or nearly so. Are we supposed to pray for that driver as well as the accident victim?

Jesus wanted us to give justice and mercy to those around us. On our own it's almost impossible. Only by truly giving ourselves to God, walking in His footsteps and by the power of the Holy Spirit, can we love and pray for people who wrong us, and see them through His eyes. Ask God to deliver you from self-involvement and to help you reveal His love to the world around you. Ask the Holy Spirit to place love in your heart for all people, even the unlovable, and see what happens to your comfort zone.

NOTES

NOTES

Cruising with the King

...so that they [the priests] may offer sacrifices pleasing to the God of heaven and pray for the well-being of the king and his sons (Ezra 6:10).

When faced with crucial decisions, high-ranking government officials often pray at the opening of their sessions. Soldiers, fighting to protect this country from terrorism, pray before they go out on a mission. When someone is dying or severely hurt, prayer is an accepted form of comfort, even by those who have never uttered a real prayer in their lives.

The most hardened bikers will not turn down prayer from someone they've come to respect. Earning the right to intrude into a biker's life is crucial, and it's not something that just happens overnight; it's a long process of building trust. Bikers who minister to other bikers have worked hard, building a friendship of unconditional love, a love that Jesus displayed when He walked among us.

Look around. What do you have to offer when a mechanic at a gas station wants to look at your bike? What about the biker dude who pulls up to the pump across from you? Someone driving a cage with four, eight, or eighteen wheels will not get his attention, but you, another biker, will. You already know people who could use God's intervention in their lives. Who will show them who God really is if not you? Who will take the time to pray for them?

NOTES

Someone has prayed for every new believer long before they hear the good news. Pray for the people you will meet when you travel. The work of salvation is God's, but our task is to pray that God will soften that heart. We can approach people with confidence because God goes before us. Make sure your walk is close to God so others will see Jesus in you, so they will be open to hearing how much God loves them. Prayer can make a difference.

NOTES

Defensive Riding

On reaching the place, he said to them, "Pray that you will not fall into temptation"
(Luke 22:40).

Knowing that He would soon leave them, Jesus asked His disciples to pray for the strength to resist the temptation to run away or deny Him in the days ahead. Bikers have to ride the roads defensively too. They need to protect themselves from the temptation to speed, to drink and drive, and many other obstacles that could take their life.

Roger decided to go to a restricted biker rally. He wanted to party, to experience the freedom to do as he pleased. When he walked through the gate, vendors of temptation were everywhere. He began to drink again, a problem he'd solved years ago. One night, while under the influence, he did a burn-out on the road in front of one of the rally organizers. He'd broken their rules. The next morning some people found him very badly beaten and took him to the hospital.

Prayer can surround us with a cushion of protection when the enemy prowls around like a drooling, hungry beast seeking to kill and destroy. Satan's deceptive lies strike as arrows, no matter where we are living, what work we do for a living, or what circumstances we face. Prayer girds us with the power to discern truth from fiction, and gives us the strength to keep our priorities straight.

NOTES

The importance of binding ourselves with prayer at the beginning of each ride or rally, to wrap ourselves in prayer, like well-worn leather, makes sense. Slip on the helmet of God's protection before you face an angry biker. When tempted to act surreptitiously because you think no one knows you at that rally, pray, seek His face, and then walk in His Holy Spirit the rest of the day.

NOTES

Band of Brothers

I urge you, brothers, by our Lord Jesus Christ and by the love of the Spirit, to join me in my struggle by praying to God for me (Rom. 15:30).

Hatchet rode with some dastardly dudes. On purpose. He planned to win every one of them over to Christ's side before he died or they did. He never compromised his faith, ever. They respected him, but their lifestyle changed very slowly. In fact, it was years before there was even a glimmer of hope that Hatchet was making a difference. He drew his strength from the people who attended his home church, people who knew the dangers he faced, people who believed that what he was doing was what God had appointed him to do.

Hatchet, like Paul, asked his prayer partners to pray by the name of our Lord Jesus Christ. Paul recognized the part Jesus plays as intercessor before the Father and how important it is that our prayers be filtered through Him. Paul also asks us to pray by the love of the Spirit, since he knew that without the Spirit in us, love is at best a dismal counterfeit of the real thing.

God calls some to be missionaries, some to attend motorcycle rallies, and some to enter prisons and minister to the inmates.

NOTES

But everyone is called to pray. The prayers of believing Christians undergird the people in the trenches. Prayer gives them strength to clean port-a-potties and pick up garbage, or the wherewithal to make a healthy meal out of a food supply that they are unaccustomed to in a foreign country. Prayer can give bikers courage to enter the walled confines of prison to share the gospel with tough, hardened souls who would rather spit on them than talk. Prayer places us before the throne of God.

Do you pray for those who are in the trenches of spiritual warfare? Make a list and diligently place these people before the throne of heaven on a regular basis. You don't need to understand exactly what is happening in their lives at any given moment. Just pray when the Spirit guides you, and you will make a difference in the life of the warrior, as well as in your own life

NOTES

Tattoo the Image

I have not stopped giving thanks for you, remembering you in my prayers. I keep asking that the God of our Lord Jesus Christ, the glorious Father, may give you the Spirit of wisdom and revelation, so that you may know Him better (Eph. 1:16 – 17).

John knew the road he was traveling would someday lead to his death. Either he'd drink himself to death, or he'd lay down his bike for good one day. His best friend had changed: Billy told him he had Jesus tattooed on his heart and that's why he didn't drink anymore. The difference was that Jesus was imprinted where no one could see him. But John could see the changes in Billy's life, and he wanted those changes in his life too.

In writing to the Ephesians, Paul stated how important it is to know Jesus Christ personally—to have Jesus tattooed on his heart. People the world over know about Jesus Christ. Most respect Him as a man, a prophet, and a good person, but they do not know Him. If they did, that relationship would change their life, just like it did Billy's.

"I keep praying. …" Paul prayed that people would take the time to study the Bible, to discover who Jesus is and develop a personal relationship with Him. Paul prayed that God would reveal the truth of the Scriptures, and that the Holy Spirit would impart His wisdom into their lives.

Jesus Christ changes lives. Have you heard how skeptics seek to disprove the Scriptures, only to realize that Christ is who He says He is? They find Jesus in the Old and New Testament; they learn who He is and how to live according to His example.

Pray for the people you connect with every day, as Paul did. Do you know that you may be the only Christian in that person's life? It's an awesome responsibility but a job God has given us the tools for in His Word. What are you going to do about it?

NOTES

NOTES

Secret Council

But when you pray, go into your room, close the door and pray to the Father, who is unseen. Then your Father, who sees what is done in secret, will reward you (Matt. 6:6).

In Matthew Jesus taught many things about prayer and praying. He instructed us in the Lord's Prayer, but before he did that He told us not to pray like the hypocrites, who pray publicly so people will think they are better than they really are. Instead He tells us to find a quiet corner, a secluded spot away from prying eyes, where we can close the door on the world and all its distractions.

Grant was attending a bash. He'd been praying for his friends for some time and knew their activities this day also needed the Lord's intervention. He quietly walked toward a deserted shed located near the back of the property where the party was happening. Out of sight he bowed his head. He asked God to protect him from temptation, but he also asked God to soften the hearts of his friends and to help them make wise choices.

Have you ever gone for a solitary walk on a quiet country road very early in the morning? The sun has just peeked over the horizon. Hardly a leaf flutters in the still air, but the birds chirp their good morning chorus to each other in harmonious greeting. God's creative genius fills our souls with His love for us, and we wonder how He can love such sinners. Yet His love is all around us.

Find a quiet spot where you can enjoy His creation, His love, and His Word, maybe under a large tree or on the back deck, maybe in a specially decorated corner of your bedroom. Worship our Lord where only He can hear. This personal retreat is a place where we can be alone with Him to ask for His forgiveness, where we can receive His counsel. Our little corner of the world allows us to bask in His blessings, as we remain quiet and listen to His answers for life's problems. Reflect on His goodness, humility, and compassion, character traits He wants us to display to others. Meditate on the Word, and memorize verses from Scripture.

NOTES

Motorcycles come with maintenance manuals. So do we. The Bible, God's instruction handbook to us, contains directives to live the kind of life He wants for us. It contains truth to help us get to know our Savior better but also to help us walk daily with Him. We can't possibly learn all that those pages contain if we are not studying the Bible regularly.

NOTES

Seek the Experts

Then He opened their minds so they could understand the Scriptures (Luke 24:45).

When Jesus walked with His disciples, teaching them about the Father, He taught them from the Law of Moses, the Prophets, and the Psalms. He opened their minds so they could understand, a job that has been delegated to the Holy Spirit since Jesus returned to sit beside the Father in heaven.

Erica loved her children. She also loved to ride her Honda Shadow. Its chrome glistened in the sunshine as its blue paint sparkled from the loving care she took to wipe it free from dust. When Jesus became part of her life, she decided that she needed to take care of her children more than she did her bike. That care-giving included teaching them from the Word of God, the Bible. She'd take long walks with them to point out all the beauty in God's Creation. She made games out of Scripture memorization and prayed for their day with them every morning. She also took them to church and encouraged them to study the Bible as she now did on a regular basis.

When we open the Scriptures, the Holy Spirit is our interpreter. He helps us to understand what is written so that we can

NOTES

learn as He reveals His truth to us. Studying the Bible, working hard to understand what God wants us to know, takes time, but it is the best time we'll ever spend each day. We need to ask the Holy Spirit, before we begin reading, to reveal His truths, to open our minds, and to give us clarity of thought so that we can understand, as Jesus' disciples did, when God speaks to us through His Word.

Bible study involves research, learning from those who have studied the Bible for years. Motorcycle riders consult many people before, during, and after they've learned to ride a bike. They talk with mechanics to learn the workings of their bike, and they read the manual from cover to cover. They take rider-education courses and safety courses. When you embark on a study of God's Word, consult the one who can interpret those words, His Holy Spirit.

NOTES

Study the Manual

When he takes the throne of his kingdom, he is to write for himself on a scroll a copy of this law, taken from that of the priests, who are Levites. It is to be with him, and he is to read it all the days of his life so that he may learn to revere the Lord his God and follow carefully all the words of this law and these decrees and not consider himself better than his brothers and turn from the law to the right or to the left. Then he and his descendants will reign a long time over his kingdom in Israel (Deut. 17:18-20).

Any king in Israel had to be a man of God's Word. He was to make a copy of the law, keep it with him always, read from it daily, and obey it completely. This would help him respect God, resist feeling more important than the people around him, and avoid neglecting his relationship with God.

Josiah, or Joe as most of his buddies called him, carried a small Bible with him wherever he went. It was in the right saddlebag, alongside his rain gear and extra gloves. When he was traveling alone, every time he'd stop for a break, he'd take it out and work on his Scripture memorization or read a new passage. Sometimes, if he was riding with friends, they'd tease him, but just a little because they respected his desire to be a better man.

The only way to know what God wants from us is to study His Word. God's Word will change our lives, but only if we read and think about it regularly. In the above passage the king had to make a copy of the Scriptures. All we have to do is pick one up at our local bookstore or order it online. Then we can take it wherever we go.

Following the directives in the Bible is challenging. The people we meet like to brag about their independent spirit, their freedom of choice. Relying on a Holy God is not what they strive for, and yet there is more freedom in living as a Christian than not. Begin today to sharpen your knowledge of God's Word. Memorize whole passages and meditate on the words found within the pages of this bestseller. When you are tempted, use those memorized passages to fight the temptation.

NOTES

NOTES

Bible Culture

[Moses] said to them, "Take to heart all the words I have solemnly declared to you this day, so that you may command your children to obey carefully all the words of this law. They are not just idle words for you – they are your life. By them you will live long in the land you are crossing the Jordan to possess" (Deut. 32:46-47).

Moses urged the people—those who escaped from Egypt and were about to enter the Promised Land—to think about God's Word and teach it to their children. He reiterated that it meant their life. God's Word transforms, builds our relationship with God Himself, and builds healthy relationships with the people we meet every day. It provides fuel to fight temptation, encouragement as we minister to those around us, and promises we can count on.

What good are our motorcycles if all we do is store them? Jeremy loved his motorcycle. He'd polish it every day, sit on it, and then cover it up to sit toward the back of his garage. Jeremy would bring his friends out to see his motorcycle, but he had no interest in riding the bike. It just gathered dust and needed another coat of wax.

Like a motorcycle relegated to the back

NOTES

of a garage, the Bible does no one any good sitting on a bookshelf gathering dust. It needs to be a vital part of our lives as we set aside regular time for study. Digging through the pages to find God's wisdom is invigorating. It makes us want to apply His truth to our lives and teach it to others. We become motivated to walk in Jesus' footsteps, treating people the way He did when He walked among us. It encourages the best from us as we learn to appreciate what Jesus went through for each of us individually.

Set aside time for regular study on a daily basis. Maybe you can join a small Bible study group and work on a book together, or maybe your church offers adult Sunday school with a particular biblical topic of discussion and study. If not, purchase a Bible study and a leader's guide from a bookstore or online. Study it in the quiet confines of your home. There are also correspondence courses available online. However you choose to do it, the habit is easy to make or break, so keep at it and your life will be changed forever .

NOTES

Blurry Vision

Do not merely listen to the word, and so deceive yourselves. Do what it says. Anyone who listens to the word but does not do what it says is like a man who looks at his face in a mirror and, after looking at himself, goes away and immediately forgets what he looks like. But the man who looks intently into the perfect law that gives freedom, and continues to do this, not forgetting what he has heard, but doing it – he will be blessed in what he does (James 1:22-25).

James, the brother of Jesus and a leader in the early Church, wrote this epistle on Christian living to confront, challenge, and call his readers to commitment. James' concern for persecuted Christians outside Jerusalem is well documented; he exposed hypocrites and taught the right way to live as a Christian.

This passage addresses people who sit in church Sunday after Sunday, hearing the Word of God but not putting anything they hear into practice. While listening is important, it is much more significant to obey what it says. Ben drank a great deal last night, and this morning when he awoke, he couldn't remember what he'd done, who he'd been with, or where they'd gone. It was as if last night had not happened. That's the way it is with some people who attend church; it's as if it hadn't happened because nothing made an impression on their lives. They couldn't remember any of it.

God's Word was written to transform our lives and, through us, the lives of the people we meet. As we ride we encounter people who need a word of kindness or someone to pray for them. God's Word keeps us aware and sensitive to our surroundings. We've been fed spiritually from the Scriptures, so we are able to feed or care for others.

Each morning open God's Word and ask the Holy Spirit to open your mind to understand and incorporate what you are reading and learning. Allow the words of Scripture to change your attitude and behavior. Practicing God's Word sensitizes you to His leading as you encounter hurting souls when you ride.

NOTES

NOTES

Brotherhood of Believers

When the king heard the words of the Book of the Law, he tore his robes. He gave these orders to Hilkiah the priest, Ahikam son of Shaphan, Acbor son of Micaiah, Shaphan the secretary, and Asaiah the king's attendant: "Go and inquire of the Lord for me and for the people and for all of Judah about what is written in this book that has been found. Great is the Lord's anger that burns against us because our fathers have not obeyed the words of this book; they have not acted in accordance with all that is written there concerning us (2 Kings 22:11-13).

King Josiah was the leader of the pack. He'd read the Law of Moses, the Bible, and decided to institute some new rules for the gang. He believed these new rules were in everyone's best interest, so he made them law. With just a short time in office, things became very different for the bikers who rode in his kingdom. You see, with just one reading, King Josiah became a believer and changed the course of a nation. Yet we read God's Word repeatedly but make little or no effort toward change. Few are affected by the truths in God's Word as Josiah was.

Studying God's Word, delving into the passages with an open mind, should cause us to take action, to immediately reform our lives to bring them into harmony with God's will. But we go through the motions, pretending He doesn't know that our hearts are just the same as they were when we began. Nothing has changed.

God sees our heart condition. He knows whether our attitudes and behaviors are different or whether we are playing make-believe, putting on a good face for those around us. We can't pretend to know how to ride a motorcycle—just like we can't pretend to be a Christian in God's eyes. God has the power to send us to hell for all eternity, while people only have the power to make our lives miserable here on earth, a short blink in the eternal timeframe.

Study His Word and take it to heart; your heart will change and God will rejoice. Forget about trying to impress the people around you. The only person worthy of our efforts to make a good impression is God Himself. He sees the garbage stored in our hearts, the stuff the people around you can't visualize. He also knows how clean as snow He can make us through His Word. Take His Word to heart, won't you?

NOTES

NOTES

Bad Company

Consider now: Who, being innocent, has ever perished? Where were the upright ever destroyed? As I have observed, those who plow evil and those who sow trouble reap it (Job 4:7-8).

Eliphaz rode the bike next to Job's, pretending to be his friend, but Eliphaz was not a true friend. He did not proclaim truth to Job but half-truths, promoting sin and trouble. Eliphaz wanted to make himself look important by spouting bad theology, but Job wasn't buying his argument. Job knew that eventually people who promote half-truths, who distort the Word of God, will be punished.

What makes this passage important? All Scripture is integrated into God's Word by God's choice, but not all examples are meant as illustrations for us to follow. Eliphaz is not an example for us to follow, but Job is. Sin, defeat, evil thoughts, and misconceptions about God are all part of His divinely inspired Word, but we shouldn't copy those wrong choices just because they are in the Bible.

The Bible gives us insight into what we should do as well as what we should not do. Eliphaz was making false assumptions based on his own experience, a graphic illustration of what we should not do. Eliphaz thought he knew what was right from the little he'd studied of the Scriptures, but he only knew a small part of the things God has for us in the pages of His Word. Eliphaz assumed his interpretation was correct—which just goes to show what assuming can do.

Study God's Word to get a clear picture of right and wrong. God is not a god of gray areas. He does not allow fence-sitting. You either do what He says is right, or you do what He has pronounced wrong. Ask for the Holy Spirit's intervention as you study and pray about the choices you make—before you make them .

NOTES

NOTES

Bonds of Trust

For the Word of the Lord is right and true; he is faithful in all he does (Ps. 33:4).

Years ago, when she was a new Christian, Alyssa looked up to and admired her new friends. She envied their upbringing in loving Christian homes and the opportunity they had to attend Bible camp as children. Alyssa's home had been anything but loving. Abuse, anger, and a general lack of love from her parents marked her childhood memories. The people around her seemed to have it all together. They worshipped God, she thought, from a place of understanding who God was and what He had done for them. She felt she was beginning with three strikes against her and a long way to catch up.

Then disaster happened. Those very Christians fell off that pedestal Alyssa had placed them on. Her heroes in the faith had slipped. She stood in shocked horror as they grouped together and left the church one Sunday, never to return. Alyssa considered walking away from the hypocrites she'd admired, from the church, and from her belief in God.

When we focus our attention on people, we will always be disappointed. People are sinners, no matter how long they've been walking the path of a Christian. People fail miserably time and again because they are not perfect, just forgiven. God is the only true, righteous Being. His Word is true and right. God will never fail us, nor will He turn His back and walk away from us. God's Word is as relevant today as it was when it was written, and it should always be the book of choice when we seek wisdom.

Begin today to remove your eyes from the sinners around you and focus your attention on God Almighty Himself. Learn to see people through His eyes of love and compassion, understanding that they may fall, but God in them does not. Read the Scriptures, study His Word, and filter everything else through the constant truth found within those sacred pages.

NOTES

NOTES

One Track Mind

I am a stranger on earth; do not hide your commands from me. My soul is consumed with longing for your laws at all times (Ps. 119:19-20).

Whenever Todd leaves for a road trip on his Valkri, he takes a map along so he can find his way. The map is his guide to state parks where he will camp for the night, to city byways where he can avoid the traffic congestion, and to many other pieces of information that make his trip a safe and enjoyable one.

The Bible is our map and our guide through life. David asked God in these verses not to hide His commands. David admitted he was a stranger on this earth. Since our home is in heaven, we too are strangers, here but for a short time. God's Word is our guide through life. It shows us the way while we are waiting to enter the gates of heaven.

God's map, the Bible, needs to be studied so we don't lose our way, just as a map is studied before we make that once-in-a-lifetime cross-country trip we've always dreamed about. We need to carefully select roads that will take us around hazardous territory, the same as we need to select and memorize verses to take us past temptations or hazards on our Christian walk. We need to develop

NOTES

a thirst for God's laws to keep us on the straight and narrow pathway, just as we research the laws of the states we travel through. If Todd left his map at home, in all likelihood he would not find his destination. It is the same for us. If we leave our Bible sitting on the coffee table or a bookshelf to gather dust, we will miss our real objective, heaven.

Commit to a time each day for regular Bible study. Developing a good habit is always a challenge; Bible study is no different. Plan, read, study, and begin all over again tomorrow. Eventually you'll have established a lifetime habit that you won't want to miss. Bible study will become as common for you as breathing.

.

NOTES

Club Rules

Oh how I love your law! I meditate on it all day long. Your commands make me wiser than my enemies, for they are ever with me. I have more insight than all my teachers, for I meditate on your statutes. I have more understanding than the elders, for I obey Your precepts (Ps.119:97-100).

David learned to love God's laws, his club rules. To become part of the gang, there are rules that we adhere to. We learn them and obey them. David spent time studying, meditating on, and memorizing Scripture with the knowledge that God's Word made him wiser than his enemies, his teachers, or the elders in his life.

These same Scriptures, the ones David held in his hands, are available to us today when we open the Bible. But true wisdom does not come from knowledge alone. It comes when we apply what we've learned to our lives to change our attitudes and behavior. Jeremy purchased a new Honda Gold Wing in a magnificent shade of orange. When he got it home, he polished it until it sparkled, but he also read the manual that came with it. He spent hours pouring over the pages to learn the intricacies of this particular motorcycle.

When he took his wife for their first ride, Jeremy applied the wisdom he'd gleaned to make their ride safe and comfortable. Reading our Bible provides us with the knowledge that we can relate to different situations as we come to them. The seeds of wisdom are cultivated when we change our attitudes and behavior based on what we've studied. We allow God's Word to infiltrate our thinking.

Jeremy learned some new things about his latest motorcycle that he didn't know before, but as the days wore on those things were no longer new but became part of his thinking. He no longer had to concentrate to remember what he'd learned; it was just there. Bible Study is like that. Take the time to study, meditate, and memorize daily so you won't have to work to remember what God wants you to do in this situation or with that problem. You will just know.

NOTES

NOTES

Lights for the Road

Your word is a lamp unto my feet and a light for my path. I have taken an oath and confirmed it, that I will follow your righteous laws (Ps. 119:105-106).

Veteran motorcycle riders understand that cars, vans, and trucks cannot see them on the highway as easily as they can see a four-wheel vehicle. So the manufacturers are making the newer bikes with running lights that stay on all day and illuminate the bike. The tail-lights flash or maybe the headlamps flash, but even then, owners attach additional lighting to increase their visibility.

In our world darkness is pervasive. Evil lurks around every corner, waiting to steal, kill, and destroy. God's Word is our lamplight. It lights up the dark corners, illuminating our path with wisdom, truth, and knowledge so the evil one will not succeed in his mission.

The Bible reveals the entangling roots of false values and philosophies that tend to trip up our thinking. It helps us not stumble over temptations that come from all manner of sources, including our closest friends. The Bible gives us the strength to remain true to our faith in God and true to His purpose for our life.

NOTES

Dinah was visiting with some of her biker buddies one evening when a friend asked her to come to his apartment for a private drink. Dinah remembered that God was watching. She also remembered that God wanted her to keep herself pure until marriage. She'd learned these truths from regular Bible study. Her answer was no. Keep yourself on course with a time of personal study today.

NOTES

Peer Pressure

This is what the Lord says: Stand in the courtyard of the Lord's house and speak to all the people of the towns of Judah who come to worship in the house of the Lord. Tell them everything I command you; do not omit a word (Jer. 26:2).

God's directive to Jeremiah was clear. He was not to leave out anything God had told him to say to the people of Israel. He could have been tempted to do just that since God's words would not make him a very popular man in the eyes of his peers. Sometimes we are tempted to omit parts of the Bible as irrelevant, unpopular, or politically incorrect. God's Word, from cover to cover, is as relevant today as it was when it was written.

Dan watched as his friends partied. He kept quiet when they drank barrels of booze and then jumped on their bikes to ride like the wind. He swallowed his words when they walked off into dark corners of the yard with one of the babes brought there for just such a time. He wanted to fit in, even though he didn't plan to participate in their activities. He didn't want to hassle his peers.

God is also not concerned with political correctness or with offending one group or another. His Word crosses barriers with truth and honesty. It may not be popular to consider someone wrong for living unmarried with their significant other, but God's Word is very clear on that subject, as it is on any topic you care to research within its pages. The consequence of wrongdoing is obvious.

There are many times when words are not necessary. A changed life says it all, but if someone should ask for your opinion, a door has opened. Be bold. Walk through with God's light to shine in the dark places and God's love to soften a hardened heart. Don't change or soften God's Word; it is still relevant today to teach, equip, instruct, and illuminate.

NOTES

NOTES

Truth or Fiction

"Let the prophet who has a dream tell his dream, but let the one who has my word speak it faithfully. For what has straw to do with grain?" declares the Lord. "Is not my word like fire" declares the Lord, "and like a hammer that breaks a rock in pieces?" (Jer. 23:28-29).

Jeremiah heard God when He told him to be faithful to preach His Word to the people of Israel. God was fed up with dreamers who tried to influence people because of some vision they claimed to have. God's Word can change lives; it profoundly affects those who follow it.

Rebecca believed in psychics; at least in one she'd been going to for some time. This person just knew so much, and many of her visions came true. Her friend Daniel began sharing from God's Word when they'd meet at motorcycle rallies. The simplicity of the gospel messages and Daniel's excitement for the truth found within the pages of the Bible began to make a difference in Rebecca's life. Straw has no nutritional value for animals, but grain will strengthen their bodies and cause them to grow strong. The same is true of dreams; they have no value. But God's Word will make us strong in our faith and give us the armor we need to protect us from the enemy.

NOTES

Sharing God's Word with others brings with it a great responsibility. The way we present it and live it will cause others to either accept or reject it. We need to communicate accurately, and we need to make sure our lives depict the words we are speaking. If God's Word has changed our lives, then people will notice and desire a change, but if there's no evident change, why would others even want to listen?

When you walk through a motorcycle rally, let people see your changed life. Unconditionally love everyone you meet. When you see someone hurting from the loss of a friend, share Jesus' love with them. Let them know God cares. Sharing the love you've received from the Lord, as well as your material possessions, with no strings attached will do more to further the gospel of Jesus Christ than any words you may speak. Your life will earn you the right to speak, and then you must speak truth in love.

NOTES

Code of Truth

The tempter came to him and said, "If you are the Son of God, tell those stones to become bread." Jesus answered, "It is written: 'Man does not live on bread alone, but on every word that comes from the mouth of God'" (Matt. 4:3-4).

Knowing Scripture and obeying it will arm us against the enemy's plot to steal, kill, and destroy. Jesus knew this and used Scripture to thwart the plans of Satan. After fasting for forty days in the desert, Jesus was hungry, but when Satan suggested that because Jesus was the Son of God He could turn the stones into bread, Jesus quoted Deuteronomy 8:3. The Bible says we can use God's Word as a sword in spiritual combat. Knowing Bible verses will help us resist the devil's attacks and follow God's desires for our lives, but we also need to obey the Word as well. Satan memorized Scripture, but he failed to obey it.

Jomi spent time every day memorizing God's Word, studying the Bible, and praying to her Savior. When she rode her motorcycle one day with some other Christian bikers, they were invited to attend a birthday bash held by a local outlaw group. Jomi thought she would have an opportunity to share the gospel, so she accepted.

NOTES

When they arrived the mood was boisterous, and booze flowed from large kegs like a mighty river. The only other beverage available was water from an outdoor tap that looked none too clean. Jomi remembered 1 Peter 1:14, a verse she had committed to memory the week before: "*Do not conform to the evil desires you had when you lived in ignorance.*" She filled her water bottle with water from the tap.

Did anyone notice? You bet they did. Did they condemn her for it? No, they respected her decision to live the life she had spoken to some about at other events. They knew, just as Satan knows, that she was supposed to act differently than they did. Take some time to memorize Scripture as you study God's Word today.

NOTES

Patch Wearers

A good tree cannot bear bad fruit, and a bad tree cannot bear good fruit. … Thus, by their fruit you will recognize them (Matt. 7:18, 20).

Every Sunday David sat in a class taught by a man he respected. This man's colors were what David hoped to wear some day. Thursday, when he was riding his motorcycle through town, David spotted that same man coming out of a bar, weaving noticeably. David decided the colors this man wore (his fruit) were not something he wanted after all. He chose to attend another class.

The Bible is very clear about the responsibility of teachers of the Word. They are to live lives that exemplify the words they teach, and those words must be true to the Scriptures, not perverted to justify their own lifestyle. Their lives and behavior speak loudly about what they really believe. Jesus called the teachers bad trees, people who teach false doctrine. We are to examine their motives, the direction they are taking, and the results they are seeking.

Although we are still sinners, we must walk as forgiven sinners who show mercy to others, the same mercy we need ourselves. So rather than condemn this teacher, David chose to attend another class. But he also chose to hold this man accountable until his life conformed to the words he taught.

Discernment is a large part of walking as a Christian. Study the Scriptures so you can use God's Word to filter everything you hear, say, or do. Your actions, your words, and the things you allow to infiltrate your brain need to pass the test of God's truth. Before you can do a good job discerning what's right and what isn't, you need to know the Scriptures

NOTES

NOTES

Test of Endurance

Heaven and earth will pass away, but my words will never pass away (Mark 13:31).

Rekter collapsed on the park bench. He took a long look at his pride and joy, a 1996 Harley Low Rider parked by the curb, and then he hung his head. The news this morning had not been good. Many were calling it World War III, and he knew all about war. Rektor had fought in the Gulf War, and it had changed him forever. He knew how fragile a city, even a country, could be when nuclear weapons or chemical weapons were used. War had removed his sense of ever being safe again.

Terrorists, bombs, earthquakes, drought, flash floods, tsunamis, tornadoes, hurricanes, and many other disasters shake the very foundation of our sense of security these days. Hate-filled men, willing to sacrifice their life for what they believe, are a hard enemy to fight. Yet, brave young men are doing just that. They work from dawn till dusk and beyond to quell the tide of terrorism in our world today. Before 9/11 people in the Unites States considered themselves safe as long as they were on American soil. No more.

The Bible says that heaven and earth will

pass away. In His Word God instructs us not to place our faith in the tangible, material things we see around us, but in His Word alone. He promises that His words will never pass away; they will stand the test of endurance. Nothing, not terrorists, not floods, or any other disaster, can take His words from the hearts of His people.

So how do we lean on His Word? How do we replace our sense of security in the world with sanctuary in God's Word? We memorize, read, and study. We instill within our hearts, engrave on our souls, the very Scriptures He has promised will never leave us. When we watch the news on TV or listen to the calamities outlined on the radio, we search our hearts and receive comfort, knowing that God is still there and loves us, the same today as He did yesterday and the day before that.

NOTES

Jesus left His disciples with one command. He told them to go and make disciples of all nations. He did not give this as a suggestion; it was a command. Sharing our faith with others can be intimidating if we compare ourselves to the great theologians in our time. Jesus did not just ask great theologians or great evangelists to make disciples. He asked us all, ordinary people meeting with ordinary people, biker to biker. This next section may help spur you toward that goal.

NOTES

Family First

Moses told his father-in-law about everything the Lord had done to Pharaoh and the Egyptians for Israel's sake and about all the hardships they had met along the way and how the Lord had saved them. Jethro was delighted to hear about all the good things the Lord had done for Israel in rescuing them from the hands of the Egyptians (Exod. 18:8-9).

Spider knew the Lord, and as he parked his chopper inside the garage, his thoughts turned to his wife and children. They knew something was different about him. He hardly ever swore any more, and he worked at being kinder and gentler. His wife seemed to look at him these days with a complete lack of understanding, but she didn't turn away his help in the kitchen either. His children walked on eggshells when he was in the room, waiting for the "old man" to appear once more. It was time to tell them about Jesus.

Telling our family about our faith is sometimes harder than sharing with a complete stranger. They've taken the brunt of our bad behavior, so they are very suspicious when we try to share how Jesus can make a difference. Often they fear the loss of the old ways, while at the same time glorying in the new. Change of any kind can be threatening.

Moses began with his father-in-law. He told Jethro all the Lord had done for Israel and for him. That's a good place to begin with our own families: Simply share what God is doing in your life. It may take a while, but soon your children, wife, and extended family members will see that the changes taking place are permanent. They may even begin to trust that what you say is true, and they too may decide to give Jesus a chance.

Look for ways to open your family to the opportunities of Jesus Christ. They are the closest people in your sphere of influence, your first mission field. Gather your family and, with regular devotions, Bible study, and prayer, slowly begin to share with them some of the changes you've noticed in your own behavior and understanding. Love, real love, God's brand of love, can do wonders in opening a heart hardened to the gospel of Jesus Christ .

NOTES

NOTES

Around the Campfire

He said to the Israelites, "In the future when your descendents ask their fathers, 'What do these stones mean?' tell them, 'Israel crossed the Jordan on dry ground.' For the Lord your God dried up the Jordan before you until you had crossed over" (Josh. 4:21-23a).

Joshua built a memorial of twelve stones to mark the place where the Israelites crossed the Jordan on dry land. It was a monument to what God had done in their lives. This pillar of stones would spark questions from children in future generations. Then their parents and grandparents could tell them all God had done for them.

Denny knew the exact date when his tall, tattooed frame had bent in submission to Jehovah God. He also knew when he stopped drinking and when he smoked his last weed. His life had taken on an entirely different focus. While not piling up a bunch of stones to commemorate those dates, he had marked them in his Bible so that when he looked, he'd never forget what God had done for him.

At a recent motorcycle rally Denny decided to share those dates with a fellow biker. This man hadn't known Denny before he'd met Jesus, but he respected the man he'd become and his decision to abstain from drinking and partying with the rest of them. Denny took him to a quiet place, opened his Bible, and simply told him how God had cleaned up his life, how much better he felt, and how his relationship with his wife had changed.

That's all we're asked to do: Share what God has done in our lives and then reflect God's love to those we meet. Look for opportunities today. Ask God to soften the hearts of the people you'll meet, prepare them for your words, and see how His amazing love will transform them. Join Him where He's already working. Open your mouth, and speak from your heart .

NOTES

NOTES

Role Models

I have been reminded of your sincere faith, which first lived in your grand-mother Lois and in your mother Eunice and, I am persuaded, now lives in you also (2 Tim. 1:5).

Timothy was the first second-generation Christian mentioned in the Bible. A godly mother and grandmother raised him and shaped his life. They promoted his spiritual growth before he began to work with the Apostle Paul. Timothy became Paul's protégé and the pastor of the church in Ephesus. In the verses above Paul was reminding Timothy of his heritage.

Sharing Christ's love, helpfulness, and joy with the members of your family is an important responsibility. Jester quietly lived his life among his brothers and sisters, his parents, and his grandparents. Their small town buzzed with life, and the local bar was the place to gather every night. But not for Jester—not any longer. They teased him, but his silence left them perplexed.

One night he decided to share why he no longer enjoyed the raw humor, foul language, and smoke-filled atmosphere of Billy Bob's Bar and Lounge. He stood tall as he told his neighbors how he met

NOTES

Jesus, how the Christ of the Bible had changed his life. His friends smiled. They knew it must have been something like that.

One the way home that night Jester was able to lead one brother and a sister to Christ. He started the godly heritage that Timothy had grown up with right there on that street corner. Over the next few years, his parents, grandparents, and a few nieces and nephews also surrendered to Jesus. Don't be afraid to speak the truth. Watch God in action as He begins to work in your whole family, one person at a time.

NOTES

Type Casting

Before the spies lay down for the night, she went up on the roof and said to them, "I know that the Lord has given this land to you and that a great fear of you has fallen on us, so that all who live in this country are melting in fear because of you. We have heard how the Lord dried up the water of the Red Sea for you when you came out of Egypt, and what you did to Sihon and Og, the two kings of the Amorites east of the Jordan, whom you completely destroyed (Josh. 2: 8-10).

Rahab was a prostitute. She was a Canaanite and a pagan, but she was also interested in God. She was willing to risk everything she had for a God she hardly knew. But she understood enough to know that the God of the Israelites was not an ordinary god. The stories that had circulated through Canaan spoke of the Israelites successes because of their God, and the people of Jericho were afraid. Because of Rahab's limited understanding of and respect for this foreign God, lives were saved.

Matty was appalled. Why would Christians want to go to a place like that? A group of Christian motorcyclists sat in her living room and told stories about different rallies. Bikers, Matty thought. Why would someone care about those

NOTES

hardened criminals? And what about the drugs and drinking? When she heard them mention nudity, her mouth dropped open.

Then one speaker, with tears in his eyes, told how his very sad life had changed because Jesus cared enough to die for sinners, and Matty cringed. She'd believed that all her life. Deepdown she knew Jesus loved that man and the bikers at motorcycle rallies just as much as He loved her. He'd died for them too. How could she not care?

The people we meet, whether pumping gas or making a purchase at a convenience store, all need to know Jesus cares for them. We are His "arms and legs," and we supply the tangible love to men and women around the globe and at motorcycle rallies. Do you see people's sin instead of looking at them through the eyes of Jesus? God's heart melts when sinners finally come to understand His saving grace. They don't know that they don't know—until we tell them. Then see how different a biker's life can be.

NOTES

Black-Listed

Then they said, "The God of the Hebrews has met with us. Now let us take a three-day journey into the desert to offer sacrifices to the Lord our God, or He may strike us with plagues or with the sword" (Exod. 5:3).

Nearly everyone knows the story of the Israelites' exodus from Egypt. Pharaoh had a hard time believing anything Moses and Aaron said because he did not know or respect their God. His advisers taunted Moses, saying, "He may strike us with plagues or with the sword," and that is just what God did.

Moon used every opportunity that crossed his path to share the gospel with the men he rode with. Some listened, but others began to avoid him, taunting him with names like "Bible Thumper" and "Jesus Freak." Men who had partied with him for years now sneered at him and traveled without him whenever they could. They made him feel very unwelcome most of the time.

Moon should not have been surprised. If men could reject Jesus when He walked among them, why wouldn't they also reject His message of grace? Moon began to pray earnestly for each of his comrades by name. He asked God to soften their hearts, to open their minds to the freedom they could experience as Christians. Moon continued to love them. He did not take their rejection personally. Over the years two of his best friends accepted Jesus as their personal Savior, and others learned to respect his faith, even if not accepting it for themselves.

When people reject the message of hope found in the pages of the Bible, we need to stand firm, continue to tell them, and trust God to do the converting…in His time. Consider those around you. Do you pray regularly that God will touch them? Begin today to make a concerted effort to include them in your daily talk with God. Ask God to soften their heart and provide you with an open door as well as the words that will point them in the right direction .

NOTES

NOTES

The Ultimate Promise Keeper

Noah did everything just as God commanded him. The Lord then said to Noah, "Go into the ark, you and your whole family, because I have found you righteous in this generation (Gen. 6:22 – 7:1).

As Willie contemplated the fate of his friends, he had trouble sleeping. His neighborhood Bible study revolved around the topic of the end times and God's coming judgment. He read verses that spoke of hell and the antichrist. His friends didn't know any of this—or did they? He remembered Freddy making jokes about the party they'd have when they all got to hell one day. Another time Josh spoke about Armageddon as if it were just another war. Maybe some of them did know. Then why were they still on such a destructive path, rejecting the very idea of a holy God?

Some people talk about disaster in their lives but really don't expect it to happen to them. In Noah's time God told everyone He would flood the earth. Only Noah believed Him and set to work constructing an ark that took him years to build. Everyone else wasted their time taunting Noah about building a boat in the middle of the forest, not even close to a lake or any other large body of water.

Today thousands of people are warned of God's inevitable judgment, yet most don't really believe it will happen. They see floods, hurricanes, tornadoes, earthquakes, and tsunamis but still reject the message of the Bible. In some cases they try to inspire other Christians to also reject that message of doom and gloom in favor of a God of love. While God does love us unconditionally, He is also a just God who will carry out His sentence of destruction on those who reject Him.

Do you know someone who looks at world events and wonders what's going on? That could be the open door God has placed in your path to share Jesus with them. Begin today to share His promise of deliverance from the judgment that is sure to come. Remember Noah and God's promise to keep him safe. God keeps His promises. That we can count on.

NOTES

NOTES

News for the Dying

Then they said to each other, "We're not doing right. This is a day of good news and we are keeping it to ourselves. If we wait until daylight, punishment will overtake us. Let's go at once and report this to the royal palace" (2 Kings 7:9).

Cade's motorcycle broke down with only half the distance across the desert completed. His water bottle was empty and so were the bottles of his traveling companions, five other bikers of varying shapes and sizes. The gas tanks on two bikes were nudging empty, and a third had overheated just before they'd stopped. There was no one in sight—no cars or houses and hardly any trees to shelter them from the intense heat.

Cade decided to walk for help. He trudged over the dusty road, completing a hot, sweat-filled mile. He rounded the bend, and there in the middle of nowhere was a convenience store. He ran the rest of the way, opened the door, and stepped into cool, breezy comfort. He bought a large bottle of cold, refreshing water and drank his fill, enjoying the break from the heat. Cade languished in comfort, preoccupied with his own needs. He completely forgot about his friends.

Sometimes we forget about sharing our

NOTES

message of hope. We forget people are dying without it. We become consumed with our faith, studying the Bible for ourselves, keeping the message hidden from the very people God has placed in our path for that purpose. The Good News of Jesus Christ will not wait until a more convenient time. Our biker buddy may die the next time he rides.

Consider your sphere of influence, those people you've already built a relationship with, the very ones God has given you responsibility for. Are you waiting for the right time? A better time? A more convenient time? Now is the time. Tomorrow may be too late .

NOTES

Some Ride, Some Don't

The couriers went from town to town in Ephraim and Manasseh, as far as Zebulun, but the people scorned and ridiculed them. Nevertheless, some men of Asher, Manasseh and Zebulun humbled themselves and went to Jerusalem (2 Chron. 30:10-11).

TJ was diligent in sharing his faith. Every time he traveled to a rally, participated in a poker run, or met his biker buddies filling their gas tanks, he shared Christ's love with them. He prayed with the ones who would let him and performed little acts of kindness whenever he could. TJ behaved toward his friends—and those he met on the highways and byways—as he knew Christ would if He rode a Harley.

Some mean-spirited bikers ridiculed TJ and his faith. They made jokes about his choice of drink when he entered a bar during a poker run. One big old biker even tried to trip TJ when he came out of the bar to make everyone think he was drunk. Several times TJ returned to his motorcycle to find mud splashed all over it or beer poured on his custom leather seat.

However TJ was making a difference. People watched as he held his temper when he was tested. They watched him go out of his way for this person or that one. They also watched his continued sense of peace when their hearts were in turmoil, and peace was something that was foreign to most of them. One day TJ had the privilege of leading a fellow biker to the Lord. That, he thought, made everything he'd endured worthwhile.

What do you do when you're ridiculed and mocked for being a Christian? In 2 Chronicles Hezekiah had sent messengers to offer the people an invitation to the Passover. Many mocked him, but several accepted the invitation. Many will mock your invitation from Christ, but some will accept. Don't give up. Keep on spreading the Good News, and someday your efforts may be rewarded, although there are no guarantees. It is enough that you are being obedient to Christ's command, and He will take care of the rest.

NOTES

NOTES

Earn the Right

Esther had not revealed her nationality and family background, because Mordecai had forbidden her to do so (Esther 2:10).

For twelve years, several Christian motorcyclists attended a rally where they worked hard cleaning showers, picking up garbage, handing out water, and doing just about anything they could to develop a relationship with the others in attendance. Few opportunities for a clear witness presented themselves—they thought. In fact, some gave up and began attending other events instead.

Benny was one man who went back year after year. He smiled all the time and looked for opportunities to show Christ's love instead of saying the words. As the years passed the bikers he met at this rally began to watch for him to arrive. They began to look for excuses to be with Benny and to sit by his campsite. They were drawn to this man who never spoke an unkind word about or to anyone.

That's what Esther did when she became queen. She waited for the opportunity to share who she really was, but until that opportunity presented itself she was quiet. Her uncle Mordecai had forbidden her to reveal her nationality, but by the time danger came to her people, Esther had earned the right to tell her king who she was. Consequently the Jewish people were saved from annihilation.

Sometimes it takes a long time, but we must earn the right to speak about Christ. We can show His love, but trust has to be earned. Is there some way you can earn the right to speak to the people God has placed in your path? Maybe you see them only once a year. Will they remember you as a kind person and someone they can trust, or will they remember you differently? It's up to you.

NOTES

NOTES

Under the Leather

On the first day, Jonah started into the city. He proclaimed: "Forty days and Nineveh will be overturned." The Ninevites believed God. They declared a fast, and all of them, from the greatest to the least, put on sackcloth. When the news reached the king of Nineveh, he rose from his throne, took off his royal robes, covered himself with sackcloth and sat down in the dust (Jon. 3:4-6).

Jed was a biker, and he believed he was a Christian. He wore brown leather instead of black so no one would identify him with those outlaw types. He was careful to avoid the places many of them congregated. He thought he was better than they were. After all, he didn't drink, do drugs, or spend time in jail.

His friend Josh did exactly the opposite, much to Jed's annoyance. Josh purposely shook hands with, talked to, and hung out with as many black-leather-clad bikers as he could. He got to know the person under the leather. He found out they were not so very different from his friend Jed or himself. They all had families and jobs just like he and Jed, and they all paid taxes. Sure, one or two had been in a scrape with the law, but for the most part, the black-leather guys were just normal, everyday people.

NOTES

Josh had more than once shared his faith with these tough-looking men, just as he had with Jed. But Jed needed none of what Josh was selling…or so he thought. Jed looked the part, but his heart condition left a lot to be desired. Josh's other biker friends cared about what he had to say once he'd earned the right to say it. Hungry spirits, who understood they had fallen short of God's perfect plan, received his message. No one needed to tell them they were sinners. They knew they'd made mistakes. They longed for peace and forgiveness.

Get past the outward appearance, just as Jonah did when he finally shared God's message with the Ninevites. Jonah knew about the vicious people who lived in Nineveh, and he incorrectly prejudged their reaction to God's message, for they did repent. When God places someone in your path, don't look at who you think they are; look at who God knows them to be. Love them as He does, and see what happens.

NOTES

Pipe Lure

People went out to him from Jerusalem and all Judea and the whole region of the Jordan. Confessing their sins, they were baptized by him in the Jordan River (Matt. 3:5-6).

John the Baptist had an audience. He dressed differently than his contemporaries, ate a special diet, and preached about a coming Savior. He baptized in the Jordan River, a ritual that was common among the Jews who used it to initiate converts. However, John preached repentance and only baptized repentant sinners who chose to believe John's message of salvation. People were drawn, not only to him, but to his message.

People are attracted to motorcycles. Loud burps from throttles of bikes with customized pipes roar down the street, chrome glistening in the sunshine. A classy finish makes each bike distinctive and entices onlookers to stop and stare. They dream of someday riding with the wind in their hair and the splendor of nature surrounding them. People see strength and power not only in the machine but also in the rider, resplendent in black leather. A motorcycle rider has an audience, whether he wants one or not. His actions can cause fear or can help people feel comfortable with his leather-clad demeanor.

Patch decided, after becoming excited about his newfound faith in Jesus Christ, to use his motorcycle as a tool, something to entice people to hear his message. He rode with purpose and continued to enjoy his experience, but with a different motivation. He spoke about Jesus' love to anyone who listened. And people paid attention.

God opens doors. He uses whatever is at our disposal to influence the lives of the people around us if we simply walk where He walks and share the words He has placed on our heart. Today take a step into the palm of God's hand. Let Him lead you toward those whose hearts have already been touched with the Father's love, those who need to know that Jesus loves them. Give them the opportunity to turn control of their life over to the Lord.

NOTES

NOTES

Circle of Friends

As Jesus was walking beside the Sea of Galilee, He saw two brothers, Simon called Peter and his brother Andrew. They were casting a net into the lake, for they were fishermen. "Come, follow me," Jesus said, "and I will make you fishers of men." At once they left their nets and followed Him (Matt. 4:18-19).

Peter and Andrew had met Jesus through John the Baptist who testified that He was the Son of God. In John 1:35-42 John told about how Andrew knew Jesus to be the Messiah and about how he shared that knowledge with his brother Simon, whom Jesus renamed Peter. In Matthew, when Jesus asks them to follow Him, they did not follow blindly. They knew enough about Jesus to trust and respect Him. They believed He was the long-awaited Messiah. Jesus invited them to join Him in ministry.

Jesus' invitation is extended to each of us. Denny listened. At work he modeled his Christian belief, earning the respect of the guys in the department. Occasionally one of them would ask him to pray for a sick child or a marriage in turmoil. One day someone asked him to explain why he had such peace in his life, and he was able to lead a hurting man to the Lord.

NOTES

When Denny purchased his first motorcycle his world of influence broadened. Now other bikers talked to him when he was filling his bike's gas tank. They waved when he passed them as he rode down the highway, and they invited him to join in the fun at some rallies nearby. Denny wasn't sure what to do. He'd heard enough to know that most Christians would not be caught dead at one of those rallies, and yet…

Denny prayed and studied God's Word. He began to see the hurt evident in these new friends. He also began to experience God's love for them, to understand that God died for them, just as He died for regular church-attending people. He knew they didn't know what they didn't know about Jesus, and that God had placed him in their lives for just that purpose.

Each person has a ministry, a sphere of influence different from any other person. If you won't tell your friends about Jesus, who will? If you get to heaven one day and the Lord asks you about Digs, Johnny, or Bugs, will you be able to look Him in the eye and say you were faithful? Will you be able to tell the Lord you planted that seed into a life so He could water it and make it flourish? Or will you hang your head in shame, knowing that if Jesus walked the earth today, He'd be where the bikers are, loving them, and pointing them toward heaven?

NOTES

Mistreated

"Be on your guard against men; they will hand you over to the local councils and flog you in their synagogues. On My account you will be brought before governors and kings as witnesses to them and to the Gentiles" (Matt. 10:17-18).

Patch's leather vest sported a large logo on the back declaring his allegiance to the biker group he called family. It also contained a round circle with the "1%" sign that most of his buddies also wore with pride. He wore his hair and beard long, taking pride in the freedom to dress as he pleased. His bike of choice had ape hangers for handlebars, and the front forks extended farther out front than when he'd first purchased it.

One day, Patch added another emblem to his vest. It was a cross. He didn't say anything to anyone, but before long many of his friends began to look at him differently. They talked *about* him, not *to* him. They were wary around him, sending him a message that they didn't trust him anymore. Patch began to feel alienated, not part of the group any longer. Some even voted to remove his back patch, to kick him out of the club.

Jesus warned His followers that they would be persecuted for His sake. Patch had decided to follow Jesus. He'd turned his life over to His Lord, drinking soda pop instead of beer and cleaning up his language. He even began to do nice things for the other guys and invited one or two to join him in church on Sunday. Patch became a different person on the inside. He learned that Jesus had overcome the world when He died on the cross, making it possible for His followers to withstand the harshest criticism and persecution.

When you are faced with opposition, ridicule, or snide remarks because of who you've become since meeting the Lord, remember that in some countries people are actually put to death for their belief. Continue to love your persecutors, for one day they may also turn their life around because of something they've seen in you or someone else

NOTES

NOTES

He'd Have Ridden a Harley

"Why does He eat with tax collectors and 'sinners'?" On hearing this, Jesus said to them, "It is not the healthy who need a doctor, but the sick. I have not come to call the righteous, but sinners" (Mark 2:16b – 17).

Christine was appalled. How could Christians go to that place? She listened as her biker friends talked about the activities that occurred at some rallies and wondered about the strength of her friends' belief system. It almost sounded as if they were fence-sitting, keeping one foot in the world and pretending to be Christians the rest of the time. They even went to bars on poker runs!

Christine would probably have agreed with the Pharisees when they questioned Jesus for cavorting with tax collectors and sinners. She was comfortable in her pew every Sunday, separating herself from the world and the very people Jesus came to save—sinners. She didn't want anyone to see her with that woman down the street who had three children from three different fathers, or with the dirty, unkempt man who roamed the streets looking for odd jobs so he could afford a decent meal.

If Jesus were walking this earth today, instead of mingling with tax collectors, he'd probably wear leather and ride a Harley, a tool to open the biker world to His message and love. He'd walk into the midst of them, loving them but not participating in their games. He'd help them in any way He could, earning the right to draw them to Himself. He'd remember that it was for such as these that He'd died in the first place.

God has placed one, maybe two or more, people in your path so you can minister to them, not ignore them. You are His hands and feet. You are the visible body that people see before they can come to know the Savior who is in your heart. You are the extension of His love to everyone, not just the ones you deem worthy. Who have you been avoiding lately? Maybe God has called you for just that person. See that one through Jesus' eyes, and share His love with that needy soul today.

NOTES

NOTES

Blackballed

"I tell you, whoever acknowledges me before men, the Son of Man will also acknowledge him before the angels of God. But he who disowns me before men will be disowned before the angels of God (Luke 12:8-9).

Cheryl looked around her bedroom. Pretty pink curtains fluttered in the breeze coming through the window as she took off the dress she'd worn to work that day. She tugged on black leather pants and a cream colored t-shirt, and then slipped on her vest. A large, colorful patch that told the world she was a Christian adorned the back of the vest. Cheryl decided to take off the patch. She intended to go to a party that night and enjoy herself. She didn't want people thinking she was a goody-two-shoes. She didn't want anyone there to know she was a Christian.

In the book of Luke Christ says whoever lets people know He is their friend, He will also call them friend before God's angels. But a person who pretends not to know Jesus in public will be disowned before those same angels. You either are a believer or you are not. Walking with the Lord means strolling in His foot-steps, hour by hour, day by day, at home or away.

NOTES

There are many ways we can disown Jesus. Besides trying to hide our Christianity, when we fail to speak up for what's right or when we prefer to blend into society and accept our culture's non-Christian values, we turn our backs on the sacrifice Jesus made for us on the cross. Christ says he will blackball us, disown us, just as we refuse to acknowledge Him before our peers.

Resolve today to live a moral, upright life. Look for ways to share Christ's love with others and to help those in need. Take a stand for truth and justice, and use your life to carry out God's plans, not your own. Wear His colors with pride.

.

Sharing your faith with another is an act of obedience to God. But simply left to their own devices, new believers may be snatched away by the circumstances in their life that have not yet changed. We have a responsibility to help strengthen them. Discipling those with new faith is like watering plants that have not yet taken root in new soil. Making sure their spirit is fed regularly is the only way to ensure their walk with God will overcome their circumstances, and not the other way around .

NOTES

Last Will

Therefore go and make disciples of all nations, baptizing them in the name of the Father and of the Son and of the Holy Spirit, and teaching them to obey everything I have commanded you (Matt. 28:19 – 20).

Before Terry took off for a cross-country bike ride, a trip that would last most of the summer, he made out his will…just in case. In this document he outlined how he wanted his family to respond should he have a serious accident, and he gave them directions about where to dispose of his possessions.

People make out living wills, as well as after-death wishes, all the time. For the most part, their relatives and friends listen and do whatever they've been asked to do. Jesus also had a serious request to make just before He ascended into heaven. He asked His disciples to go into the entire world, make disciples, and baptize them. He asked His faithful followers to teach these new converts everything He had taught them.

To make disciples wherever we go is not a suggestion; it is a command. If we are to be obedient, then we will do as Jesus requested. But we're not supposed to just share our faith and then leave our listeners to their own devices. Jesus also said

NOTES

we are to teach them. That requires us to build an ongoing relationship with new believers, to act as their spiritual parent, and to teach them to also go into all the world to make disciples—to be obedient to Jesus' words.

Begin today. Look for a neighbor, a friend, someone placed in your path who will die a sinner if you don't share your faith with him. You may be the only Christian in that person's life, or you may be one of many, but do what Jesus commanded. Fulfill your role as that person's life vest. And then take that person under your wing. Help him find a good church. Begin to study God's Word with him so that some day he will go out and find the person God wants him to disciple.

NOTES

Sissy Bar

Then the disciples went out and preached everywhere, and the Lord worked with them and confirmed his word by the signs that accompanied it (Mark 16:20).

Jeremy was a new believer. His motorcycle club members watched him closely to see if he would step off this new path he'd chosen. They blew smoke in his face, accused him of thinking he was better than them, and paraded scantily clad women before him constantly. He walked out of the bar and sat on his bike. He watched the moon light up the night sky and felt all alone.

Then he leaned back, placed a hand on his sissy bar, that backrest he'd installed just three months ago so his passengers could ride a little more comfortably. He remembered the Bible verse from Mark, a study he'd embarked on last night with some Christian friends. The verse told how Jesus supported His disciples, like that sissy bar supported his passengers.

Jeremy smiled. Jesus was with him even when he met with his biker buddies. Christ had given him a mission: share his faith with his friends. Christ walked beside him in this mission, just as He did when He sent His disciples out. Jeremy walked back into the bar, grabbed his can of pop, and smiled. His mission field was all around him.

Christ gives us a mission, but He also promises to be with us in that mission. He doesn't expect us to walk the path alone. He opens doors and carries us through them, one step at a time. Stand tall in your mission, love those whom He's given you, and remember to lean on your Lord, seeking His will, His support, and His strength. .

NOTES

NOTES

Paroled

If you hold to my teaching, you are really my disciples. Then you will know the truth and the truth will set you free
(John 8:31-32).

Lucky stepped out into the warm sunshine. Nothing obstructed his vision—no bars, no gates, and no metal of any kind. He was free. Lucky took a deep breath and let it out slowly. His freedom came with a stipulation. He had to meet with a parole officer regularly. His freedom would last as long as he followed the rules.

Jesus' offer of freedom from sin comes with a stipulation as well. John 8 says, "If you hold to my teaching…" Walking in freedom is not as easy as it sounds, and while we might succeed for a while on our own, the enemy is prowling around, waiting to kill and destroy, waiting to throw us off balance and knock us off our bike—off our path to freedom from sin.

New believers need to immerse themselves in God's Word, getting to know Jesus and His truth. They need to put on the whole armor of God, memorizing Scripture to defeat Satan's attempts to wreak havoc in their life. New believers need the fellowship of other believers, as well as the spiritual guidance and group study from close friends who will hold them accountable.

Lucky had chosen to follow Christ while he was in prison. Because he did, a couple of Christian friends met him when he was released. They enveloped him in Bible study and church, and provided him with a job. They discipled him—just as Christ discipled His followers. If you've been instrumental in leading new believers into a saving relationship with Christ, don't abandon them to the world or to their own devices. Keep them accountable, and involve them in church and Bible study. Help them be successful in their Christian walk, and teach them to share their faith, just as you did.

NOTES

NOTES

Warm Fuzzies or What?

A new command I give you: Love one another. As I have loved you, so you must love one another. By this all men will know that you are my disciples, if you love one another
(John 13:34 – 35).

Jessica and her girlfriend walked out of church after listening to an inspiring sermon on love. *Wow*, she thought, *that's love*. They hopped on their motorcycles and rode home, each lost in thought. Jessica began thinking about ways she could show love to her friend.

The pastor had said that the love Christ talked about in John 13 was different than a warm fuzzy feeling in the pit of your stomach. It was an attitude that resulted in action. She thought about the many times her friend had asked her to baby-sit, or the time she'd moved into a different place and asked for help with the move. Jessica had said she was too busy, but in reality she'd just not felt like it.

Christ's love means doing things for people even when we don't feel like it. Feelings have nothing to do with it; action does. When Trudy was camping at a biker rally, another woman asked her if she had an extra towel. Trudy gave her the one she'd brought. When Dixie arrived home from work, her neighbor ran out of her house just as it exploded in flames. Dixie phoned the fire department and then took her neighbor into her home for three months while her neighbor's home was repaired.

Christ's love can be expressed in many ways, but always by actions that disregard our own discomfort, and always without complaint. He says that by this kind of love others will know we are Christians. Jessica's friend knew Jessica was a Christian in theory but had never seen it displayed in action. Trudy and Dixie's encounters pointed people toward Christ

NOTES

Just Like Me

When he [Barnabas] found him [Saul], he brought him to Antioch. So for a whole year Barnabas and Saul met with the church and taught great numbers of people (Acts 11:26).

The church buzzed with activity when Jeremy walked through the front door. He could sense that familiar feeling of belonging as he looked around, but then he noticed the changes. Several groups of people, some dark-skinned, were conversing in different languages. His church family entered into the conversations as if they knew these people. In a few short months, the length of time it had taken him to complete his job overseas, his church had taken on an international flavor.

Jeremy entered the sanctuary. More strangers, at least to him, sat in the pew where he usually parked himself. They smiled their greeting, but Jeremy didn't know how to respond as he sat down beside them. He wasn't sure this was his church anymore. As he placed his Bible on the seat next to him, he watched as the family nearby opened their Bible. During the entire service the glow from their eyes radiated their love for Jesus. Diverse cultures, yes, but Christians, just like him. Jeremy was home.

NOTES

In Antioch, when Paul and Barnabas arrived, they too noticed the different cultures represented in the church they visited. But this was the first group of people called Christians, or Christ followers. Their relationships reflected their similarities, not their differences. Paul and Barnabas continued to meet with them for a whole year.

When a biker walks into our church, do we treat him as if he belongs? Or do we look at him as if he's crashed our party, as if he's not invited? When a stranger makes his way toward the sanctuary, do we smile in greeting and offer to shake his hand to welcome him, or do we continue toward our own seat and ignore him? Our similarity in Christ is all that matters. Look to Jesus and welcome everyone into His loving embrace

NOTES

Earning Your Patch

But commission Joshua, and encourage and strengthen him, for he will lead the people across and will cause them to inherit the land that you will see (Deut. 3:28).

After Digger prayed with John he knew his job was just beginning. John had a lot to learn if he was going to survive his friends' raucous party lifestyle. But John was determined to share his faith with the people he'd hung with for years. So Digger prepared to teach, train, and mentor his new friend until John was ready to minister to the other bikers in his club, as Christ commanded.

God told Moses to do the same thing with Joshua. He was to strengthen and encourage Joshua so the younger man could lead the people of Israel into the land of Canaan. After weeks of preparation, meeting together on a regular basis and holding each other accountable, John was ready to begin his own work for Christ. Digger continued to strengthen and encourage John, as he stepped up his involvement and began to share his faith.

Discipling another believer, becoming a spiritual parent, is a commitment of time, energy, and emotional involvement. A mentor must be obedient as he seeks God's will for his own life and then car-

NOTES

ries the Great Commission to its conclusion in the life of a new convert.

John had to earn his patch when he joined his biker club. Now he had to earn the right to speak on Christ's behalf. Digger helped John along his path of discovery as he studied his Bible, coming to know God's will for his life. He began to know Christ himself. Think about the people in your life. Have you become a spiritual parent? If not, why not?

NOTES

Back-up

But the men of Israel encouraged one another and again took up their positions where they had stationed themselves the first day (Judg. 20:22).

The dictionary defines *encouragement* as "to give hope or promise." Encouragement is what the men of Israel gave each other just before they went into battle. Encouragement is what we need to give each other so we can face life's trials and tests. Encouragement strengthens us, helps us live a purposeful life. It helps us defeat temptation, try new things, and step out of our comfort zone. Encouragement is necessary for new believers.

Denny knew the boys were giving Tristan a hard time. He knew they treated his changed attitude with disdain and ridicule. But Tristan continued to associate with them anyway. God wanted him to, he said. So Denny prayed for and with Tristan every day. He encouraged Tristan's walk with the Lord by meeting with him once a week for breakfast and doing a short study together. Denny gave Tristan hope.

God wants us to give encouragement to each other all the time. Going to church offers us the opportunity to pray with people, to sense when someone needs a card or an encouraging phone call during the week. It also helps us add specific people to our regular prayer time and gives us the opportunity to ask people to be praying for a specific day or event coming up in our life.

Being a Christian is more than our relationship with Christ. It is also our relationship with the people He's placed in our lives. Simple encouragement can make or break someone's day. Listen to the Holy Spirit as He brings people to your mind. And then be obedient. Place that call, send that card, or pray.

NOTES

NOTES

Timing

Then they returned to Lystra, Iconium and Antioch, strengthening the disciples and encouraging them to remain true to the faith (Acts 14:21b – 22a).

Paul and Barnabas had been threatened and physically attacked in these towns, and yet they returned to encourage other believers. They disregarded the threat to themselves or the lack of comfort and the poor timing. They knew the early Church needed them, just as they'd needed Christ to go to the cross for them when it wasn't convenient.

Has God called you to a place where your encouragement is needed? Look around. It won't take long for you to find a hurting soul or someone floundering in their faith. Are your doors open? Can people call you when they need a word of encouragement or prayer?

Jeremy stumbled up the steps of his friend's house. The windows were darkened against the night sky. He rang the doorbell, a light came on, and then he heard footsteps. Brian scowled at him through the small glass pane in the center of the door. Jeremy hung his head, hiding the shame but pleading from his heart for Brian to understand. Brian smiled and opened the door.

NOTES

Brian hugged Jeremy and offered him a glass of cold water. Jeremy poured his heart out; he was ready. Brian was able to pray with him for the first time, a prayer that changed Jeremy from a committed sinner to one forgiven and cleansed with Christ's blood. Watch for God's timing, not yours. Keep your door open for your opportunity to supply God's encouragement and strength.

NOTES

Lifting up a Brother

I am sending him to you for this very purpose, that you may know how we are, and that he may encourage you (Eph. 6:22).

Bear walked into the room. Heads turned and a few waved to him, urging him to join their table. He stood quietly and looked into the faces of his brother bikers. So many were floating through life, no anchor to hold them, to guide them toward a better life. Bear knew he had the answer. His dilemma was how to tell them.

Bear had just come from a different kind of rally. He'd met Christians from all over the country and was amazed at the solidity of their faith in an invisible God. Bear was a new believer, but at this rally he'd grown rapidly. He heard solid teaching and received the blessing of men who loved him regardless of his background. As his faith grew his resolve to take many of his brothers with him into heaven also grew.

His fellow believers prayed with him before he left the rally. They promised to continue to pray as they sent him back to share his faith. They also sent words of encouragement so these longtime friends would know that they'd be welcome wherever other Christians gathered.

NOTES

Bear's heart skipped a beat. Could they see how different he was? Did it matter? As he stepped toward the first man he'd come to know when he'd first joined the group, he was met with a high five. Over the next week he managed to share his faith with three others.

Bear became the club's encourager. The members respected his integrity as they watched him walk with them and yet not do some of the things they did. He also didn't judge them or make them feel as if he were better than them. God had sent him, just as he sends you, to encourage and to tell others who He is and how much He loves them. Are you obedient to your call, to share your faith, to encourage believers, and to boldly walk among the people God has placed in your path?

NOTES

Getting High on God

Therefore encourage each other with these words (1 Thess. 4:18).

Pug knew his friends were reading the latest accounts of the war in Iraq. They had acquaintances who'd already returned, their lives changed, their hearts hurting in unfathomable ways. Other buddies remained in the midst of the civil unrest in that country. It had been three years, but the fighting seemed just as bad as when the troops first entered to deliver democracy to this dictatorship.

He watched the faces of his associates. They feared for their friends' lives but also feared for their own. This war was different than any other. The enemy could be living right next door and they wouldn't know it until he blew himself up in a crowded room. Dying was not a problem for these fanatics, so it seemed there was no way to defeat them. It appeared to be the beginning of the end, as they'd heard many of their fellow Christians speak about the end times.

Pug stood in the center of the room. He opened his Bible and began to relate the verses that told how we would all live forever just as Christ lived forever. No matter what happened in the world, as Christians they had eternity with Christ to look forward to. They need not despair when loved ones die or when the world seemed to be on a collision course with tragedy.

He encouraged his biker buddies with the verses about how God will turn our tragedies into triumphs, our poverty into riches, our pain into glory, and our defeat into victory. Pug comforted his friends with the promise of the resurrection, just as each of us should comfort one other. Remind anyone who asks about the promise of the resurrection and that this world will pass away, but Christ remains forever in heaven.

NOTES

NOTES

Play or Pay

Preach the Word; be prepared in season and out of season; correct, rebuke, and encourage – with great patience and careful instruction (2 Tim. 4:2).

Rattler, chaplain for the SOQ's, a biker group that held regular meetings and often rode to party and carouse, felt the sense of responsibility God had placed on his shoulders. Several members professed faith in Christ, but often their lifestyle didn't show it. Rattler intended to change that.

That morning he'd read the verse in 2 Timothy that told him he needed to be prepared, to correct, rebuke, and encourage with patience and careful instruction. He studied hard all that day and for the next few weeks, watched his friends, but said nothing yet. He prepared, worked hard to understand the verses he needed to use, the words that would convict his buddies about their poor choices. He also prayed for God's direction and timing.

One morning, ready to do battle, Rattler called a meeting of his friends. He asked them to bring their Bibles, and many groaned, but in their hearts they knew Rattler had something important to tell them. Paper was handed out, Bibles opened, and then Rattler began. He reminded them of Christ's love for them

NOTES

and of the decision they'd made not so long ago. Then he began to expound on some of their wrongdoings. The men hung their heads.

Correcting a fellow believer is not easy. Most of us, if we are honest, would rather sweep stuff like that under the rug, but God's Word is clear. We are to hold each other accountable. We are to behave in a manner pleasing to God or pay the price of separation from Him. Rattler didn't want his friends to lose their faith, to walk away from the changes they'd already begun to display. Discipling new believers takes commitment and time, but it is work God has called each of us to do. Take your commitment seriously. Hold others accountable, and accept rebuke when someone holds you to your word before God.

.

NOTES

Walk the Talk

Similarly, encourage the young men to be self-controlled. In everything set them an example by doing what is good. In your teaching show integrity, seriousness, and soundness of speech that cannot be condemned, so that those who oppose you may be ashamed because they have nothing bad to say about us (Titus 2:6-8).

Chad rode his motorcycle through town, careful to obey all traffic laws. He was well known in the business community for his integrity, compassion for others, and his sincerity. Chad modeled the things he'd learned through regular Bible study and in church. He acted in a non-judgmental way toward others, displaying Christ's love wherever he went. Chad walked the talk.

Walking the talk means to walk first, before you open your mouth, in a manner consistent with the things you want others to learn about God and the Bible. If you teach or preach one set of ideals but your conduct does not reflect what you are teaching, others will disregard your words and the Book it comes from as well as the God you profess to believe.

Paul urged Titus to be a good example to those around him. Paul's words had greater impact because he walked the talk. Paul tells Titus to be above criticism, with a quality of integrity that comes from careful Bible study. He also tells him to listen before speaking, especially when teaching or confronting others about moral or spiritual issues.

Do you walk the talk? Have you earned the right to be heard because of your lifestyle, your integrity, and your honesty? Above all, have you stepped up to the plate in the lives of the young men and women who look to you for guidance? Begin today to be the example Paul spoke about. Earn the right to lead others, to teach, and to confront, keeping others accountable, just as you are accountable to our Lord and Savior Jesus Christ.

NOTES

NOTES

Warning Signs

Things that cause people to sin are bound to come, but woe to that person through whom they come. It would be better for him to be thrown in the sea with a millstone tied around his neck than for him to cause one of these little ones to sin. So watch yourselves (Luke 17:1-3a).

Jenny knew she was responsible for her younger sister. In fact, she'd been responsible for Beth ever since their parents died in a motorcycle accident three years ago. At that time, Jenny was twenty-one, ten years older than Beth. Even with Beth living in her home, Jenny continued to party, to live life "to the fullest." Beth watched her every move. Now she was fourteen. She wanted to join Jenny when she went out. She wanted to smoke pot and drink, just like her big sister.

That night Jenny made some decisions that affected the way she dressed, worked, and socialized from that time forward. She wanted her sister to live differently than she had, so she knew she'd better clean up her act and set a good example. Jenny moved the two of them to a different neighborhood, began attending church, and insisted that Beth join her every Sunday. Beth grumbled and complained at first, but eventually

NOTES

she made some new friends and started to enjoy the youth group.

Jenny took her responsibility seriously. She'd attended church with her parents when she'd lived at home, so she knew the words Jesus spoke to His disciples about leading someone astray. Beth flourished under Jenny's new leadership, and both of them became excellent examples to other young people who came along after them.

Christ holds us accountable for the people He's placed in our lives. As Christians we are to set a solid example, learning all we can about life through the Scriptures so that no one can say we led them down the wrong path. Make sure what you are saying is biblically sound. The only way to accomplish that is through regular study. Choose your words carefully, but be open to God's leading and the teaching of the Holy Spirit so that you too can set an example worthy of your calling from God Himself.

NOTES

Not a Book of Myths

All Scripture is God-breathed and is useful for teaching, rebuking, correcting and training in righteousness (2 Tim. 3:16).

Denny shook the dust off his mother's Bible. He tossed it into a box, just as his younger brother, Ben, walked into the room. Ben bent down and retrieved the worn book. He fanned the pages and noticed several places where his mother had added some notations. He closed the cover and stroked it, remembering the times he'd seen her reverently read passages just before she left for work each day.

The two brothers were cleaning up their mother's home, in preparation for an auction the next day. They'd buried her three days before. Ben decided this book was a possession—the only one he wanted—to remember his mother by. Maybe some day he'd return to church, though he didn't believe that stuff anymore. The stories, the myths, were just that—fables. Or were they?

Two months later he decided to ask a pastor at the church closest to his home about this ancient book. The pastor told him how God, through the Holy Spirit, revealed Himself and His plan for humankind to certain men who wrote down the message so God's people could learn about Him. The pastor went on to say that the words in the Bible were useful for teaching, to scold and correct, as well as train people how to live a life pleasing to God. Ben began to look upon his mother's Bible with a different light. Eventually he began attending a Bible study so he could learn more.

If we think the Bible is nothing but a collection of myths, then we can easily dismiss the words on its pages. When we understand that each word was placed there by God Himself, the Bible takes on greater significance and meaning, something to adhere to for eternity. What do your friends say the Bible is? Begin today to dispel their mistaken theories, and show them the Bible is worthy of their time and attention. .

NOTES

NOTES

Prepare for the Ride

Always be prepared to give an answer to everyone who asks you to give the reason for the hope that you have (1 Pet. 3:15b).

During those months when the ride season is on hold because of icy streets and cold northerly winds, Rebel takes his bike apart. He cleans each piece of the motor, replaces worn or damaged parts, and then re-attaches everything meticulously so when ride season begins, he's prepared.

He also spends time studying his Bible, memorizing special verses, and reciting his testimony so he will be prepared when God sticks a new face in front of him. Rebel was filled with the hope of eternity, but he knew that some of the people he rode with despaired of ever making it to the ripe old age of sixty. Their lifestyle was dangerous, but they didn't know any other way to live. Rebel intended to tell them.

When you see your friends heading for some disaster of one kind or another, do you spend your time praying for someone else to show them a better way? Why do you think you are in their life? God has called each of us to be His voice, His love, His example to the world He's placed us in. You need to be prepared to let Jack, Jenny, and George know about your hope in Jesus Christ, and how He went to the cross for your sin and theirs so you could live free from temptation and degradation.

We spend time preparing for a safe ride season. We also need to prepare for the close encounters we will have during the time we are riding or when we are gassing up the bike. Don't let regret over missed opportunities dog your steps. Seize the openings as they come, and make the best of them as Jesus did when He walked the earth .

NOTES

NOTES

Final Chapter

Paul was a chaplain. When he began a conversation, his first question was, "Can you ever remember a time when you did something wrong?" Every person he spoke to admitted they'd committed a sin or two in their life. He agreed with them. In fact, he told them the Bible, in Romans 3:23, says, "For all have sinned." Everyone falls short of God's perfect example.

Paul also told his friends that because God is a Holy God, He's placed a penalty on humans for the sin they commit. He told them about Romans 6:23, which says the penalty of sin is death, but not just physical death. Paul's friends could accept physical death as a fact of living. They'd seen or heard about bikers going down and not ever getting up again. However, spiritual death, separation for eternity from God, was what Paul referred to when he quoted from Romans 6:23. Imagine a world without love of any kind, without peace, without truth—ever. That is complete separation from God. He is the Author of love, peace, and truth, as well as many other attributes we take for granted.

Paul handed everyone a gift. All his friends had to do was make it their own. That gift is Jesus Christ. Because God loved us, His creation, He designed a

NOTES

way for that terrible penalty of separation, of spiritual death, to be paid. He came to earth in the form of a human child, and then died as a man on a cross. He paid the price for the sin we all commit. He willingly allowed Himself to be beaten and broken in a most horrible way. Because of His sacrifice for us Romans 6:23 says, "…the gift of God is eternal life" (with God, instead of eternal separation from Him). When our physical body dies, we step into the presence of God to bask in His love forevermore.

Paul explained that God did not wait until we deserved that gift. He paid it while we continued to sin. Romans 5:8 tells us that while we were sinners, Jesus died for us. Then, from Romans 10:13, Paul gave everyone his own personal invitation to accept that gift of eternal life with God, forgiveness of sins now and the power to live this life to God's glory here on earth. The Bible says, "Whoever will call on the name of the Lord will be saved." Will you open your arms to receive this gift from God, through the words of the Apostle Paul, today? Will you finally step over the line separating you from God and take your first step of faith by receiving Jesus as your personal Savior?

God does not expect you to clean up your life first. He knows every sin you have committed and every sin you continue to commit. He only asks you to let Him do His job. Let Him clean up your

NOTES

life so subtly that you won't even know its happening until one day you look back and see how far you've come.

Paul wrote in Romans 10:9-10, "If you confess with your mouth Jesus is Lord…" In other words, if you declare your allegiance with God's motorcycle club and "believe in your heart," you will be saved. God is the only one who knows what is really happening in your life all the time. He knows when you become His child and mean it. He knows what your heart condition is. Will you give God the right to become the leader in your life, to become the ultimate boss man in everything you do?

If he was standing here today, Paul would tell you that you are in this place for a purpose. It is no accident that you are reading these words right now. God is calling you, inviting you, to become His child, to join the club. Will you accept that invitation now? Let's pray….

Father God, forgive me. Cleanse me from the inside out. I ask Jesus to become the boss man, the leader, the ultimate controller of my life. Please help me to live according to Your purpose for my life, for now and evermore.
AMEN .

NOTES

Further Study

Anger:

James 1:19-20 –	Everyone should be quick to listen, slow to speak and slow to become angry for man's anger does not bring about the righteous life that God desires.
Proverbs 29:22 –	An angry man stirs up dissension, and a hot-tempered one commits many sins.
Matthew 5: 22 –	But I tell you that anyone who is angry with his brother will be subject to judgment.

Forgiveness:

Daniel 9:9 –	The Lord our God is merciful and for giving, even though we have rebelled against Him.
Micah 7:18 –	Who is a God like You, who pardons sin and forgives the transgression of the remnant of His inheritance? You do not stay angry forever but delight to show mercy.
Matthew 6:14-15 –	For if you forgive men when they sin against you, your Heavenly Father will also forgive you. But if you do not forgive men their sins, your Father will not forgive your sins.

Forgiveness:

Acts 26:17b-18 – I am sending you to them to open their eyes and turn them from darkness to light and from the power of Satan to God, so that they may receive forgiveness of sins and a place among those who are sanctified by faith in Me.

Adultery:

Matthew 5:28 – But I tell you that anyone who looks at a woman lustfully has already committed adultery with her in his heart.

Hebrews 13:4 – Marriage should be honored by all, and the marriage bed kept pure, for God will judge the adulterer and all the sexually immoral.

Faithfulness:

Psalm 31:23 – Love the Lord, all His saints! The Lord preserves the faithful. But the proud He pays back in full.

Galatians 5:22 – But the fruit of the Spirit is love, joy, peace, patience, kindness, goodness, faithfulness, gentleness and self-control. Against such things there is no law.

Faithfulness:

1 Corinthians 10:13 – No temptation has seized you except what is common to man. And God is faithful; He will not let you be tempted beyond what you can bear. But when you are tempted, He will also provide a way out so that you can stand up under it.

Drunkenness and Gluttony:

Proverbs 23:20-21 – Do not join those who drink too much wine or gorge themselves on meat, for drunkards and gluttons become poor, and drowsiness clothes them in rags.

1 Corinthians 5:11 – But now I am writing you that you must not associate with anyone who calls him self a brother but is sexually immoral or greedy, an idolater or a slanderer, a drunkard or a swindler. With such a man do not even eat.

Ephesians 5:18 - Do not get drunk on wine, which leads to debauchery. Instead be filled with the Spirit.

Self-Control:

Proverbs 25:28 – Like a city whose walls are broken down is a man who lacks self-control.

1 Thessalonians 5:7-8 – For those who sleep, sleep at night, and those who get drunk, get drunk at night. But since we belong to the day, et us be self-controlled, putting on faith, and love as a breastplate, and the hope of salvation as a helmet.

I Peter 1:13 – Therefore, prepare your minds for action; be self-controlled; set your hope fully on the grace to be given you when Jesus Christ is revealed.

Dissension:

Galatians 5:19-20 – The acts of the sinful nature are obvi ous: sexual immorality, impurity and debauchery; idolatry and witchcraft; hatred, discord, jealousy, fits of rage, selfish ambition, dissensions, fac tions and envy; drunkenness, orgies, and the like. I warn you, as I did be fore, that those who live like this will not inherit the kingdom of God.

Romans 13:13-14 – Let us behave decently, as in the day time, not in orgies and drunkenness, not in sexual immorality and debauch ery, not in dissension and jealousy. Rather clothe your self with the Lord Jesus Christ and do not think about how to gratify the desires of the sinful nature.

Unity:

Psalm 133:1 – How good and pleasant it is when brothers live together in unity!

John 17:22b-23 – They may be one as we are one. I in them and you in me. May they be brought to complete unity to let the world know that you sent me and have loved them even as You have loved Me.

Colossians 2:2 – My purpose is that they may be encour aged in heart and united in love, so that they may have the full riches of complete understanding, in order that they may know the mystery of God, namely, Christ. those who live like this will not inherit the kingdom of God.

NOTES

NOTES

NOTES

Feedback

Which part of this book did you like the best?

____

____

____

____

____

Would you be interested in another devotional for bikers? ______

How has this book helped you? ____________________

____

____

____

Name: (optional)______________________________
Address:____________________________________

Please send to : Eaglesnest Publications, 106 Leander St., #40, Alta, Iowa, 51002

Additional copies can be purchased by visiting www.barbaraannderksen.com